ᖃᔅᓯᑦ?
QASSIT?
HOW MANY?

ᑎᑎᖅᑐᒐᖅᑐᖅ
ᐊᒫᓐᑕ ᓵᓐᑦᓚᓐᑦ

TITIQTUGAQTUQ ILLUSTRATED BY
Amanda Sandland

ᐊᑕᐅᓯᖅ ᕿᐱᒃ.

Atausiq qipik.

There is one blanket.

ᒪᕐᕉᒃ ᐳᐊᓘᒃ.

Marruuk pualuuk.

There are two mittens.

ᐱᖓᓱᑦ ᐅᒥᐊᑦ.

Pingasut umiat.

There are three boats.

ᑎᓴᒪᑦ ᑐᒃᑐᑦ.

Tisamat tuktut.

There are four caribou.

ᑕᓪᓕᒪᑦ ᐅᖅᑲᓕᒫᒐᑦ.

Tallimat uqalimaagat.

There are five books.

Nunavummi